PRAISE FOR YURI HERRERA

"Yuri Herrera is Mexico's greatest novelist. His spare, poetic narratives and incomparable prose read like epics compacted into a single perfect punch—they ring your bell, your being, your soul."

Francisco Goldman

"Yuri Herrera must be a thousand years old. He must have travelled to hell, and heaven, and back again. He must have once been a girl, an animal, a rock, a boy, and a woman. Nothing else explains the vastness of his understanding."

Valeria Luiselli

"My favorite of the new Mexican writers."

John Powers, *NPR Fresh Air*

"Playful, prophetic, unnerving books that deserve to be read several times."

Eileen Battersby, *Irish Times*

"*Signs Preceding the End of the World* is short, suspenseful . . . outlandish and heartbreaking."

John Williams, *New York Times*

"Herrera's metaphors grasp the freedom, and the alarming disorientation, of transition and translation."

Maya Jaggi, *The Guardian*

"Herrera packs *The Transmigration of Bodies* with the sex, booze and nihilism of a better Simenon novella."

Sam Sacks, *Wall Street Journal*

"I was captured by *Kingdom Cons*. His writing style is like nobody else's, a unique turn of language, a kind of poetic slang . . . hands from an alternative sky."

Patti Smith

BOOKSELLERS ON YURI HERRERA'S TITLES

SIGNS PRECEDING THE END OF THE WORLD

"I am in awe-filled love with its heroine: Makina is a vibrantly real presence in a shadowy world of constant threat; her voice perfectly rendered; her unflappable poise tested, but never broken."

Gayle Lazda, London Review Bookshop, London

"Herrera gives us what all great literature should – poetic empathy for dire situations in a life more complex and dynamic than we imagined."

Lance Edmonds, Posman Books (Chelsea Market), New York

THE TRANSMIGRATION OF BODIES

"This is as noir should be, written with all the grit and grime of hard-boiled crime and all the literary merit we're beginning to expect from Herrera."

Tom Harris, Mr B's Emporium, Bath

"Fabulous. An everyday story of love, lust, disease and death. Indispensable."

Matthew Geden, Waterstones, Cork

KINGDOM CONS

"*Kingdom Cons* might be his best yet. Herrera delivers a stunning example of how art can dissolve boundaries and speak truth to power."

Matt Keliher, Subtext Books, St Paul

"Revelatory. I think Yuri Herrera has created his own genre. The mix of high and low culture, the argot of the streets with the poetic narrative – it's something else."

Mark Haber, Brazos Bookstore, Houston

A SILENT FURY

A SILENT FURY

THE EL BORDO MINE FIRE

Yuri Herrera

Translated by Lisa Dillman

SHEFFIELD – LONDON – NEW YORK

First published in English in 2020 by And Other Stories
Sheffield – London – New York
www.andotherstories.org

First published as *El incendio de la mina El Bordo* by Editorial Periférica, Cáceres, Spain

The English edition is published by arrangement with Yuri Herrera c/o MB Agencia Literaria S.L.

9 8 7 6 5 4 3 2 1

ISBN: 9781911508786
eBook ISBN: 9781911508793

Editor: Tara Tobler; Copy-editor: Linden Lawson; Proofreader: Sarah Terry; Typesetter: Tetragon, London; Typefaces: Linotype Neue Swift and Verlag; Cover design: Andrew Forteath. Printed and bound on acid-free, age-resistant Munken Premium by CPI Group Ltd, Croydon, UK.

This book has been selected to receive financial assistance from English PEN's PEN Translates programme, supported by Arts Council England. English PEN exists to promote literature and our understanding of it, to uphold writers' freedoms around the world, to campaign against the persecution and imprisonment of writers for stating their views, and to promote the friendly co-operation of writers and the free exchange of ideas. www.englishpen.org

And Other Stories gratefully acknowledge that our work is supported using public funding by Arts Council England.

CONTENTS

EL BORDO

The El Bordo mine, located in the mining district of Pachuca-Real del Monte, had ten levels, each named for its depth in meters underground: 142, 207, 255, 305, 365, 392, 415, 445, 465, and 525. These could be reached via three different shafts: El Bordo, La Luz, and Sacramento, the latter belonging to the Santa Ana mine.

The El Bordo caught fire on the morning of March 10, 1920. At least eighty-seven people were killed.

Traces of this history are few: the Pachuca 1920–1966 case file, a handful of news stories, and a metal plaque that talks about something else. The file and news stories do not simply convey the events but are *fragments* of the events; they are part of the tragedy and the way its official version was imposed. In these texts there appear both favored men, who were never at risk of being so much as scratched by a prickly question, and men and women who were doomed from the outset. But there are also oral accounts, given by miners and their families, and it was through these that I learned about the fire; there are at least two *crónicas*, one by Félix Castillo, the other

11

by José Luis Islas; and a novel by Rodolfo Benavides. All were written years afterwards.

This book, like those accounts, refuses the judicial truth that reduces this history to a file in an archive. But none of these words are mine. I reconstruct the El Bordo fire using the names, dates, and events that coincide in these accounts, insofar as coincidence is possible, and where the accounts disagree I use what appears to be most credible; I also call attention to some of the extraordinary contradictions and omissions in sources from that period that contributed to a persistent silence. Silence is not the absence of history, it's a history hidden beneath shapes that must be deciphered.

THAT DAY

The bells never rang, the ones that were there expressly for that kind of event, even though, as the agent from the public prosecutor's office noted months later, they were indeed functioning properly.

There were some who later said that they first smelled smoke at two o'clock in the morning, but it was at six that Delfino Rendón raised the cry of alarm, once he had finished cleaning the chutes on level 415. He had just extracted several loads of metal on 525 when he detected an unfamiliar smell and decided to go up, and then up some more, and on reaching 365 and approaching the shaft wellhead he noticed something that smelled like woodsmoke, and that the level was too hot. He saw no flames of any kind, nor did he need to in order to know that someplace they were already licking the mine shaft, so he raised the cry of alarm. Which was more of an act than a cry, because the first thing he did was to send down the cages to get people out, and then notify the stations by telephone, telling them to inform everyone to get out now, right now, immediately. That's what he did, as any self-respecting man would have done: worry about his fellow workers before worrying about machines or stopping to wonder how this could have happened. And the cages went up and down perhaps eight times, bringing up ten miners per trip at most. Delfino kept sending down cages, which disappeared into the unbearable clouds of smoke filling the shaft, and those cages came back up, but then they came up empty.

Agustín Hernández, cager, would later say it was at the seven o'clock whistle that the fire got really fierce. But the first flames could have broken out much earlier, or perhaps they were what caused the smoke he smelled at four thirty or five, when he stopped on level 365. Still, when Hernández asked Antonio López de Nava what was going on, the deputy foreman replied, "Can't you tell? They just blasted, so the air's full of powder dust." And since he convinced himself that it must, of course, have been the blast, he paid no more attention until, at six o'clock, he smelled smoke on 415 and went all the way up to the collar to ask, but they didn't know anything about it. While he was up there, the 525 deputy foreman, José Linares, belled for the cage. Agustín descended again, and on his way down the smoke was so strong as he passed level 207 that he nearly passed out, but made it to level 525 and stayed there with Linares and his men until they were able to get almost everyone out over the course of several trips.

Linares, for his part, had spent the night working the stope with twenty-seven men, and then at six o'clock had gone down to the office on 525 to hand in his report, which was when he smelled the smoke; and from there, on level 525, he called 415, but no one answered.

Edmundo Olascoaga also smelled smoke at about six o'clock that morning, after spending his night shift working on levels 207 and 255 with ninety-four men under his command. In fact, he was on 207 when he smelled it and descended to 255 but saw nothing; he returned to 207, surveyed the level, and then went down La Luz shaft to 415, where he found López de Nava, who by this point perhaps no longer believed, as he had an hour and a half earlier, that it was just powder dust from a blast; together the two of them went up to 305, where the smoke was thicker, and then down to 392, "where the fire was" (that's what Olascoaga said, but he didn't say why, and no one else claimed to have seen flames there); and López de Nava stayed there, on level 392, to disconnect the piping. Olascoaga then returned to the surface and informed White, the administrator; they descended together to the deepest level, and on their way up heard López de Nava shouting to them but were unable to stop the cage's violent ascent. Hours later, when Olascoaga recounted all of this in his statement, it was clear that he still held out hope that López de Nava and his men were taking shelter in a crosscut that connected to the Sacramento shaft, because after he and White emerged they sent the cage back down four more times so that López de Nava could escape, but four times it came back empty.

According to J. F. Berry, the American superintendent of the company, José Linares was the last man out. Linares had called level 415 to warn them before getting his men out of 525, and he had kept calling, he said, because at the time he didn't know what had happened to the men but he did know there was still time to get them out. Until he had to stop waiting and leave with his crew.

He was the last to make it out, but not the last to try. An engineer by the name of Eduardo Cisneros said he'd seen brain matter and shredded clothing on one of the cage ropes, no doubt that of someone who'd seen the passing car and attempted to catch it on its way up to the surface.

It took very little time for the authorities to conclude that it was too late for help, even though nobody knew for certain how many miners were still underground. A company representative by the name of Silbert first said there were 400 people working, then that there were 346, not 400, and that of those only forty-two had not made it out. But by midday Berry was assuming and declaring and signing in the margins to confirm that the total number of dead was ten, because he'd seen the last worker, whose name was Linares, make it out; he also said that the fire was already out, despite the fact that carbide canisters could still be heard exploding.

It was already out, said Berry in his midday statement, and immediately thereafter explained that in order to ensure that "the fire was completely extinguished" (despite being "already out") they would hermetically seal the El Bordo shaft, and then hermetically seal the La Luz shaft, and then once there was no more smoke they'd initiate their descent from there, see what the fire had done, and bring up the corpses.

It's unclear what time it was when they decided there was no one left alive, but by noon there was already a plan in place to bring up as a "corpse" anyone still in the mine. The report in which mine administrators notify the authorities that a fire broke out and that "all possible measures were taken" to put it out lists no time, but it was received at ten minutes past eleven in the morning. In that report there is no mention of having sealed or sealing or being about to seal the mine.

Despite there being no official time when the shafts were sealed with people still inside the mine, there is one statement, taken by a reporter for *El Universal* from miner Delfino Rendón, who said that just "twenty minutes after the miners' rescue began, out of the blue the supervisors gave the order to halt operations, and the entrances were closed." This means they would have sealed the shafts at just after seven twenty, before many of the men were even aware that they needed to get out, given that it was seven o'clock when cager Agustín Hernández, who was in charge of getting people down and bringing them up, confirmed that the smell was indeed smoke.

(It would take days for them to verify the exact number of men still inside, and of those they would never learn how many were still alive when the shafts were sealed. Yet in very little time they managed to calculate what it cost to have the mine closed: soon after the fire, Mariano Soto, an engineer who saw to the affairs of mine owner Andrés Fernández – "a Spanish tycoon," as *Excélsior* called him – told *El Universal* that this was "not some common mine fire but a very serious incident whose ramifications cannot yet be measured." He then went on to declare that the mine extracted 14,000 tons of metal per month, valued at 500,000 to 600,000 pesos, and that it would take three months, minimum, for normal production to resume.)

So the shafts were sealed at seven twenty, or at ten, or at noon, or at four. And Judge Manuel Navarro ordered an investigation, but not about that, not about who closed the shafts or at what time, or what criteria the administrators had used to ensure that the last miners made it out, but about the cause of the fire. That was the purpose of the preliminary investigation opened in the very hours when they might have reasoned the most pressing question was how many people could still be alive inside the mine. But the decision to begin the investigations with this other objective came about in what seemed almost a natural fashion, the result of a series of rational consultations.

The judge heard Berry's statement, and Berry had heard Doctors Manuel Asiáin and Guillermo Espínola, who were of the opinion that, due to the carbonic gas trapped in the mine, it could not be expected that any workers still down below at twelve o'clock were alive, since "it would take no longer than five minutes for them to die in that gas." So he authorized them to seal the shafts, which had likely already been sealed. The question as to whether the number of dead miners was ten or forty-two, therefore, was merely academic: by twelve o'clock they had already decided that all of those still underground were dead, as there was no other possibility.

Six days later, when the mouths of the shafts were opened, as promised, and they went in to bring up the corpses, not only did they discover that there were eighty-seven men – not ten or forty-two – but that seven of the miners on level 207 were still alive.

THE WAIT

A photo published on the front page of *El Universal* on March 12 shows forty-eight people (perhaps more; the image is blurry in places). Most are women wearing shawls, accompanied by boys in hats and girls also in shawls. They are staring at the camera, looking very serious. None of their faces display the scenes of desperation mentioned in the story accompanying the photo. On either side, a few men also stare at the camera while others look at the women. The caption reads: "Those waiting outside the mine for their loved ones to emerge . . . "

Another photo, at what looks to be the entrance to a mine, shows several men standing in profile or three-quarters profile. Crouching in the center, in an elegant hat, is reporter Jacobo Dalevuelta, gazing at the camera. The caption reads: "Jacobo Dalevuelta in the mouth of hell." (The stories published by both *El Universal* and *Excélsior* are credited to pseudonyms or have bylines listing only "the correspondent" or "our representatives.")

In another, about thirty men cluster together to appear in the frame. You can only just make out the faces of a few, and even then only their brows or hats. All are wearing hats, except for the five in front, who wear helmets. The caption reads: "The rescue team."

The following day's edition of *El Universal* has more photos of El Bordo. One – with a hand-drawn frame – shows a man standing before three horses and an automobile. The caption reads: "On the way to the burned-out mine."

Another, smaller, photo depicts seventeen men standing in three rows, looking at the camera. The caption reads: "The captains of El Bordo."

Another is of half a dozen coffins. The caption reads: "The victims' caskets."

There are also a few photos in the case file. The Supreme Court of Justice authorized a photographer to record the extraction of corpses. The court's law clerk, J. J. Osorio, sent a telegram to inform the court of this permission, "recommending him the greatest possible economy." The photographer took only four photographs.

The first is of the survivors; I will discuss it further on.

The second is of two corpses in a room. The room has one low window, and there are a few things off to the left that look to be ropes; it's impossible to discern what the room is used for in non-catastrophic times. The corpses are laid out on the floor, but you can only discern the face on one of them. Not its features, simply *the fact that it is a face*. On the other you can see a naked torso and not much else. These bodies are "the least disfigured" that the photographer could find. Two men crouch behind them, looking at the camera.

The third photo shows sixteen men in suits and hats surrounding a rescuer, who is the only one offering the hint of a smile. They look somber, circumspect but not troubled; one of them is smoking a cigar. They're standing before the headframe, staring at the camera. It looks as though they're very concerned about coming off in the official document like men who are undaunted, who never lose their grace despite being atop a burning grave. In the background, to the right, is another man, probably a miner, in a hat but not a suit, someone who slipped into the frame; he's holding on to the winch, and is the only man not posing stiffly.

The last is a photo of the just-excavated common grave and the men who dug it. There are twenty-six men inside the grave. All wear hats. At least five of them are holding shovels in their hands; sixteen wear face masks; eighteen are standing on top of the first coffins, which have already been deposited in the enormous grave. On the rim, above the grave, stand forty more men and one woman, also looking at the camera. The woman wears a shawl. Some of the men have bandanas over their mouths. In the background you can see the A-frame roof of one of the mine's outbuildings. In the center of the photo is a coffin, secured with ropes, about to be lowered into the grave. The elegant men from the previous photo are not to be seen in this photo: this is not their place, this is not their responsibility. Unlike the miners who dug the grave, they don't climb in even to pose.

None of these are candid photos, of course; all have been staged. The people in them remain tense as light captures them on a plate. Their paralysis is required in order to record them, but the tension is deceptive, because while these people stood frozen, everything around them was changing: the authorities were making decisions, the press was making judgments, and down below some men were decomposing while others were fighting for their lives.

On March 12, they opened the mouth of the Santa Ana, which connects to the El Bordo mine, to do reconnaissance. The galleries were littered with bodies: at the entrance alone they found forty, and the rescuers who made the descent estimated that there could be over a hundred. It was impossible to estimate, not only due to the state of the bodies but also because the examiners were forced to leave after just a few minutes down below. The smoke they encountered was still so thick that even with their helmets they felt the noxious gases were suffocating them and returned to the top almost immediately. They sealed the mouth of the mine once more, but those few minutes had been enough to reinvigorate the fire. They were also enough for them to see with their own eyes that the shaft mouths had been sealed while people were trying to escape.

During that first incursion they managed to extract only pieces of men, or what they suspected were pieces of men, charred and disintegrating, vestiges contorted into such unlikely positions that it was impossible to recognize them as human. Until it did become possible: until, after looking at them over and over and over again, they recognized their human form, in horror. The *Excélsior* reporter saw "the stiff arms of some raised to the heavens as though begging for mercy; other bodies looked to be kneeling; those farther away seemed to have lost their lives while scratching at the walls, searching for a manway to save them, and others, finally, displayed the sweet peace of those who perish without realizing that the angel of death has let his exterminating ax [*sic*] fall upon them." For some reason, one of the authorities present informed the press that there were sixteen bodies, though this number was not subsequently confirmed.

The ongoing fire notwithstanding, it was announced that the removal of bodies would recommence the following day and that the mayor would descend into the mine for an inspection. But it was not until March 15 that any courthouse official appeared at El Bordo for the unsealing of the mouths. And when Mayor Donet and Judge Navarro did arrive, Berry told them that Rose, the general manager, and Lantz, the mine manager, had decided that the mine could not be opened. That it had been a mistake to have opened it on the twelfth. That the reason they'd sealed it to begin with still held, and that if they unsealed it again the fire would reignite once more. That was what was conveyed to the authorities. Through Berry. Because

Rose and Lantz didn't show up to communicate with the authorities in person. They sent a message. And the judge, "considering these justifications," said that this was fine and ordered them to unseal the mouths the following day instead, and then turned and went back to the courthouse.

Rose made the decisions with which the authorities complied, and despite being a man of great importance, never once does his full name appear – not in any part of the investigation's case file on the El Bordo fire – nor is there any indication that he was ever called to testify.

It did cross some people's minds that perhaps the Company was in some way responsible for the tragedy. But the journalists sent by *El Universal* and *Excélsior* made sure to discredit any doubts raised and point their fingers at the miners instead. The *Excélsior* correspondent, given to voicing off-the-cuff opinions, said of the Company that "if they are guilty of neglect, which is not thought to be the case, they will be forced to pay a fine and to compensate the bereaved. In fact, the management has already spontaneously offered to do so."

He also felt that, in fact, the miners didn't care much about their own lives: "Scads of workers coming and going stared at me in surprise, as though wondering: 'Does the death of a few men really merit sending a journalist all the way from Mexico City?'" The reporter saw the mouth and face of José Linares, the same Linares who didn't get himself out until the end because he was getting his fellow miners out from one of the deepest levels, and that quick glimpse was enough for him to know the man's feelings: "He smiles constantly and shows the same indifference toward life as our ancestor Cuauhtémoc while being tortured on the rack. He even resembles him." Oh. *So he was Indian.* That's why the reporter could categorically assert that Linares's life was worth nothing, not even to Linares himself.

The *Excélsior* envoy had, on his very first visit, uncovered "the mining community's psychology":

> Here, as at similar sites, people are accustomed to staring death in the face. No one is shocked when, from the top of the mine, day after day, news makes its way down the shaft that one, ten, or fifteen have lost their lives, were injured, or are about to die. Even more than soldiers, who often believe they are destined to die each time they leave the barracks, miners are so accustomed to danger that their time-honored way of bidding farewell to their mothers, wives, and children is: "*Vieja*, I'm off to the mines. Don't know if I'll be back." And their stoicism, their indifference, their disregard for life are not feigned. In supreme moments like the one that occurred yesterday, we could see that they are sincere and come from the heart.

This same reporter claimed, on March 14, to have heard about problems between the bosses and workers, and said that miners thought to be deceased had "been seen" alive and were trying to pass for dead so that their families would be compensated – though he does not say which miners or where, only that some workers disappeared mysteriously.

A similar suspicion was held by one of the *El Universal* reporters, who on March 20 insists "it is believed" that living miners are pretending to be dead. He also quotes an unidentified Company man who, only a few hours after the fire broke out, let slip his hypothesis about its causes, as if this were the most logical thing in the world: "Perhaps carelessness on the part of the miners." The following day the same reporter quoted the (unnamed) "mine owner," who suggested that it must have been arson since the dry timbering was too far down, at least 500 meters, and the fire had been seen on one of the levels closer to 300, and in order to ignite would have required a match or cigarette butt, since the wood there would be damp, and therefore "in order to catch fire there would certainly have to have been a significant amount of fuel applied."

Whatever rumors crept in or were suggested, what the correspondents decided to see in the miners' faces was more than enough for them. The *El Universal* reporter describes how, on seeing a group of workers surface after the first incursion, he was shocked that they "emerged livid, upset, horribly affected despite their naturally indolent character." Although what he actually witnesses, what he can truly report, is the horror on the men's faces, somehow he adds, as a matter of fact, that they are "naturally indolent," despite having just met them. On the other hand, the "owner of the rich mine that burned" – Andrés Fernández, whom he also does not know, and indeed, as he himself notes, he has never interviewed – receives full personal credit for getting to the bottom of the catastrophe (although nowhere is it recorded that he was even there). The reporter expresses his joy at the fact that the tycoon is recovering: "Reports obtained yesterday about the health of Señor Fernández, who, as is known, was taken gravely ill on learning of the tragedy that occurred at his mine, are reassuring. The patient has entered a clear period of comfort." He also mentions that the owners are displeased at the judge's negligence and, therefore, Señor Fernández will appear in court as a party (he did not).

One of the many positive things reported about the American bosses was the fact that when they decided to enter the mine after the fire was extinguished, they invited the press to accompany them as a demonstration of goodwill. The *Excélsior* reporter noted that "after seeing to them exquisitely, Señores Berry, Lantz, and Rose called the journalists in to begin their work" and later, in a separate comment about the exquisite treatment dispensed, he notes that the "stance taken by the heads of negotiation, who have undertaken the removal of bodies personally, has been remarked upon in the most favorable way owing to the shining example of humanitarianism they've shown."

On the night of March 16, the judge announced that, since it wouldn't be possible to photograph all the dead, not simply because the Supreme Court had recommended "the greatest possible economy" but because the bodies that had been brought out were totally and utterly disfigured, they would photograph only one. Before finding him, it had already been decided which man would represent all of the dead: Deputy Foreman Antonio López de Nava, in whom "all of the people representing property rights in the mine" showed an interest, according to the case file.

Five days later, once the shaft was open, authorities gave up on photographing López de Nava. They still presumed him to be dead, but identifying him was impossible. Thus they opted, given that they had to photograph one body to represent the other eighty-six, to take a picture of "one of the least disfigured."

Though the photo of López de Nava does not exist, what page nine of the *Excélsior* does show is an illustration of a very distinguished-looking gentleman with a pointy mustache, tie, white shirt, jacket, and hat. Beneath him, the caption reads: "A victim of duty: Deputy Foreman Señor López de Nava," but the photo is not credited and there is no explanation as to where it came from. It is, however, reported that Olascoaga and Linares, who raised the cry of alarm, agreed that López de Nava was a "martyr of duty." *El Universal* described how, in order to save his fellow miners, he decided not to abandon the depths of the mine and instead to perish with his workmates: "The death of this man is almost glorious." José Luis Islas's *crónica* states that López de Nava had already left the mine when the fire broke out and was in a canteen awaiting his workmates, but when he heard what happened went back to help and never came out.

The March 24 edition of *Excélsior* reports that the district judge, the mayor, and an examiner of the public prosecutor's office, along with several experts, made a descent into the mine "in order to shed light on the true cause of the fire," and "of course the idea that the Company might be responsible for the fire was discarded." Because they verified that the timbering was intact and because the mine bosses had been very accommodating when it came to expediting inquiries and because they'd undertaken dangerous, arduous missions by exploring the mine in person and removing the bodies themselves and because they'd already given one bonus to the survivors and another to the workers who'd helped in the rescue mission. In reality, the only man who had descended the mine when it was first unsealed was Berry, and he was forced to exit almost immediately since the lack of oxygen nearly made him lose consciousness. There is no record of the director or manager having made any descent in these first weeks.

In the meantime, the city was left without water. *Excélsior* reported that people were pointlessly crowding around the water outlets located in the city's outskirts because the valves had been shut off since the day of the fire, when water from the dams supplying Pachuca was taken to try to extinguish it. The attempt was unsuccessful, of course – they only managed to extinguish the fire by sealing the shafts – yet in the meanwhile they'd provoked a shortage. The story noted: "There will be no water for quite some time."

THE SURVIVORS

The seven men who made it out of the El Bordo alive on March 16 were, according to the judicial inquiry, in "a perfect state of health." That's how the authorities saw them and that's how – also according to the authorities, since no statement from the men themselves is recorded – Eulogio Mendoza, Filomeno Camacho, Félix García, Fortino Pérez, Salvador Zavala, Daniel Zúñiga, and Lucio Rangel said they felt, after being driven to the Company hospital in Santa Gertrudis. There they were laid on cots and had their bodies bandaged. Then they were taken to a mining office, where the public prosecutor's examiner questioned them.

The first to speak was Félix García, who on the day of the fire was working with Daniel Zúñiga on level 255 when, at about six thirty in the morning, another miner by the name of Eulogio Mendoza came running up and asked them how to get up to level 207. Félix told him the access was by the station, and Eulogio, without breaking his stride, shouted for them to get out of there, that the mine was on fire.

They followed him, though not to the station, because by then they could see that was where the smoke was coming from, so they headed for a manway to the east. On reaching it they met two day laborers trying to get out through the same manway. They all ascended to 207, where they found two more men in the smoke, coming from the station. Trapped between two hot billows of smoke, they began racing eastward in an attempt to beat the smoke to the Sacramento shaft. They took a different manway, believing this one would save them from the fire, but after they had climbed eighty meters, it simply ended. They climbed back down and realized they could protect themselves in a raise on 207, about five meters above the drift. The smoke wasn't entering it yet, but sooner or later it would, so they sealed the raise entrance with pieces of wood, dirt, and stones. In the hours that followed, they kept removing stones to look out and putting them back, in the hope that the smoke would soon disappear, or that it had already disappeared, or that it was disappearing right then, not suspecting that they'd spend a good part of the next six days right there.

With the men on level 255 and those they'd bumped into on the way, there were nine in total. All of them had carbide lanterns, and when they realized that the smoke was not going to dissipate immediately they decided to use just one so as not to run out of fuel. They made a couple of small wells at the foot of a wall with water running down it. It was spicy, muddy water, and they thought it tasted terrible at first, but in time they got used to it.

We don't know exactly what those first few days were like, because Félix García, the sole survivor to give a detailed statement, said only – or what was recorded was only – that they'd been in almost total darkness, that they felt immense sadness, and that they lifted their spirits to God through prayer and praise.

After what they judged to be three days, the men had nearly run out of fuel. Six of them went out to survey the gallery, and on seeing that it was no longer inundated with smoke, they kept going. They came across the remains of food that some miner must have abandoned in his flight, ate his *gordas*, and combed through piles of dirt with their fingers to find stray chunks of bean. Then they continued on their way.

The men made it to a place with a hopper and a manway. One of them said that there was carbide higher up, in a different raise, which he knew because he'd been working there, and said that he'd climb up and get it. The other five told him no, said don't go, repeated no, don't go, but he took the only lantern they had and climbed up the manway. One other man followed after him. Seconds later the lantern fell and immediately went out. They tried to light it but couldn't, began shouting to the two who'd climbed up, and though they'd only gone a few meters there was no reply, nor could they hear any sounds at all. When the men realized that something terrible had happened they went back to tell the others, and it was Félix who said there had no doubt been an accumulation of gas in the raise they'd gone into, and that if the others went after them they would die too.

Later, no one was able to say what the men's names were; they knew them by sight but that was all. Indeed, Félix García's testimony is the only version of what happened, and he wasn't one of the six who went for carbide, hearing what happened from those who made it back alive. The remaining survivors said simply that they agreed with all of the details in Félix García's account.

Though by that time there was almost no smoke on 207, the seven remaining miners decided to stay in the raise where they'd survived thus far. They waited two days before emerging again, all of them together this time. The men went to the shaft station and found two miners, dead at the door. Once inside, they used paper and what matches they had left for light, and were able to see that the station walls were completely black; they tried to use the telephone but the line was down.

Then they went to the La Luz shaft, where they found things equally charred, with the phone lines there down as well. What's more, the station was full of gas and they began to feel woozy. After that they returned to their hiding place and stayed there, in the dark once more since they'd run out of matches. They lost track of the days and just waited in the dark until, countless hours later, a few went out in search of water, and that was when they felt a stream of cool air for the first time.

On March 16, at eight fifteen in the morning, in the presence of mine administrators and city authorities, the El Bordo shaft was opened once more. A dense cloud of smoke emerged. As soon as it dissipated, they stuck a lit candle on a cage and lowered it down slowly to see if there was still carbon monoxide below. Down, down, down it went, and they saw that when it reached level 305 the candle extinguished. They attempted to keep lowering the cage further still but this proved impossible: there was some sort of obstacle in the shaft on that level. They brought the cage back up, and next they put a chicken on it. Down, down, down went the cage, and they left it there for ten minutes and then brought it back up, and the chicken was still alive. And only then did Berry, Captains Palacios and Ramírez, and the electrician Paulino Aguirre descend – for a mere four minutes, just long enough to verify that the fire was out. Half an hour later, Aguirre, Berry, and Palacios went back down again, but as soon as they got out of the cage Berry fainted from the lack of breathable air, or because his breathing apparatus wasn't working properly, or out of fear, and they came back to the surface.

After ten o'clock in the morning, the engineer Quintanilla, Captain Ramírez, and Berry made yet another descent, this time through the Santa Ana shaft, to level

207. Berry stayed next to the cage while Quintanilla and Ramírez made their way through the drift.

And that was when some men — *these* men — heard voices, and other men — *those* men — felt the cool air.

At first Quintanilla and Ramírez thought what they were hearing was the echo of their own voices, but on making their way farther they were able to distinguish the silhouettes of four bodies who then stopped being silhouettes and turned into real men, who embraced them joyfully. Then they went back to the raise for the others. And then, finally, they went up to the surface.

When they emerged, the miners couldn't open their eyes. A journalist remarked that one of them was practically a boy.

The survivors were taken to the Santa Gertrudis Company Hospital, where they were examined by Doctor Espínola, the Company physician, as well as the mayor and the public prosecutor's agent, all of whom agreed that the miners were "in a perfect state of health and had no internal or external injuries," save for the fact that a few were in "an advanced state of starvation." They really said that: in a perfect state of health but starving to death. Rarely has a boss expressed so honestly what, in his opinion, the perfect worker is like. They reveled in their equal parts health and happiness, they said, after having been bathed and provided with a pair of underpants, a shirt, and a red serape. And they received no end of attention from the nurses.

That was when the men were photographed: in the photo you can see all seven survivors, barefoot, dressed impeccably in white, hands in their laps except for one, whose right arm rests on a fellow miner's shoulders. All are clean-shaven or have neatly trimmed mustaches and gaze into the camera. They don't look like they just escaped from hell: their week of underground starvation is not reflected in their expressions or on their bodies, with the exception of one, the first man on the left, who seems to betray a silent fury: lips clamped together, brows arched. But, again, no one recorded what they thought or felt at that moment.

THE WOMEN'S FIRE

Between eighty and one hundred women gathered at the mine's entrance on March 10 when they heard the double-nine, the signal indicating that something had happened. Since nobody was giving them any concrete information, they began pushing and shouting at the guards and only fell silent when a new group of miners surfaced, to see if the one they were awaiting was among them; then the last men came out and the administrators closed the mouths of the shaft.

They closed them just like that, as women were protesting. Before they did, a few of the women were still attempting to enter, though even under normal circumstances they would never have been let through, out of superstition: a woman in the mine was a terrible omen. None made it, incidentally; thus they couldn't be blamed for the fire.

The men posted at the mouths of the shaft didn't stop anyone from closing the entrance, but they did prevent the women from approaching. They no doubt assumed the womenfolk were planning to hurl themselves into the flames, as the *Excélsior* reporter speculated: "It was only the prudence and composure of a few men that saved them from being burned to a crisp."

On March 12, when they opened one shaft just long enough to go down and bring up chunks of human remains, the women were still there. According to the *Excélsior* reporter, "the throng of women and children threw themselves atop the horrific pile and, with sorrowful, heartbreaking cries of Ay!, fought as though in an attempt to earn their place in heaven, eyes popping out of their heads, arms flailing wildly, hair disheveled as they tried to hug, kiss and hold to their bosoms that pile of flesh, bones and char."

But the women in the case file seem to be incomplete, silent beings, lacking in strength and determination. The legal system turns them simply into people in need of charity – if they can succeed in proving they deserve it.

The file reports that, starting on March 12, "the Company began providing extra assistance to the relatives of the dead, and at that point the Labor Department inspector sent by the Ministry of Industry, Commerce and Labor took charge of all matters related to compensation," but it doesn't explain what this assistance was or when or how much compensation was disbursed. What does appear in detail, after many interrogations (to which the mine owners, by contrast, were not subjected), is this: the bereaved. Or, more precisely, the dozens of women related to the dead.

In the days following the fire, the miners' wives and common-law wives – and in some cases daughters, mothers, and grandmothers – were called in to give statements proving their relationship to the deceased in order to qualify for any type of compensation. Each was asked her name and occupation, whether she knew how to read and write, if she was an *untainted woman*, whether she had been the partner of the deceased and for how long, how many children they'd had; or, what her relationship to the miner was and if she had some way to prove said relationship. Every single one of the qualified witnesses called in to vouch for the truthfulness of their testimony was male.

The Prosecutor's Office questioned seventy-six people who came to assert their relationships to the deceased; seventy-three were women, but with very few exceptions none of their own words are recorded. Their statements appear only in the voice of some court clerk who interprets, edits, formalizes. One of the few voices actually heard, as though from behind bars at the courthouse, is that of María Hernández, grandmother of driller Genaro Nava, who states that she's been unable to come in to officially identify his body any sooner because she's been watching those being brought out of the mine since Tuesday in hope of seeing her son (despite being his grandmother, she is the one who raised him; to her, he's a son), and that "she was so shocked she fell sick," and thus only arrived when she did. As with many of the women who appear before the court, María Hernández has no documentation to prove her relationship, and therefore asks it to be verified through eyewitness reports.

This is the sort of document behind which flesh-and-blood relatives disappear in order to appear legally:

To the Civil Court Judge:

I, María hernández [*sic*], of San Miguel Regla, Municipality of Huascazaloya in this State, residing in house number 2 on new Gamboa street, before you respectfully affirm:

That I am the maternal grandmother of Genaro Nava, who died in the El Bordo mine fire, which took place on the March 10, on which day he passed away, but that due to circumstances beyond my control it is not possible for me to prove my relashonship [*sic*] to said man, and therefore, based on articles 1667, 1668 and others related to the Code of Civil Procedures, by means of voluntary jurisdiction I request that YOU, Your Honor:

Accept my testimony, along with the interview questions be low [*sic*], as lawful proof and provide me, in a timely manner, with the original documents required to present to the Company representative such that they grant me the compensation provided by Law.

Duly attested.

> Pachuca, March 31, 1920
> At the request of María Hernández,
> who cannot write, appended is the signature of Jesús [illegible], witness.

INTERVIEW QUESTIONS.

1. Under the oath prescribed by law, state your personal information.
2. State whether you knew Genaro Nava.
3. State whether you know me.
4. State whether you know me to be the grandmother of Genaro Nava.
5. State whether you know and confirm that when Genaro Nava died I, as his grandmother, lived with him.

Attest to the truth of your statement.

> Pachuca, March 31, 1920.
> [By hand:] At the request of María Hernández, who cannot write, signature of Jesús [illegible], witness.

A few people did have documentation. Rafaela Flores presented one certificate from her church and another from the registry office proving that she was the mother of deceased driller José Montiel, "and at her request, she will be issued a certificate of said relationship with a ten-centavo stamp owing to the notorious poverty of the concerned party."

A delayed birth certificate for Margarito Torres was accompanied by a certificate from Victoria parish legitimizing the delayed certificate, as three years earlier a band of revolutionaries had burned down the city's registry office.

Cenobio López Reyes was claimed by his grandfather, Ramón Reyes, because his parents Francisco and Eulalia were deceased and he, Ramón, had raised the boy, and when Cenobio grew up it was he who, in the words of the witness, "protected the pore [*sic*] old grandfather and kept him more or less fed." Ramón's witness was an officer from the 15th Barracks in the district of Jilotepec, more than seventy miles away; it was there that Cenobio had been born and raised.

Petra Camacho, at her hearing, presented three official documents from church and one from the San José Iturbide registry office; she said this was all she had access to there and it was noted that "due to her notorious poverty and inability to travel because of her children she was unable to return to her hometown another time to gather supporting documentation. This is what she stated, and didn't sign because she doesn't know how write." One document states that Señora Petra Camacho not be given a grave or a burial plot number for her husband because he has not been identified. In another, Petra says she was unable to be present to identify the body of her husband, José Mendiola, as she was at home "unwell after giving birth to a daughter."

Most women, however, had to confess every detail about themselves in order to exist on record:

Brígida Hernández was forced to state that she was unmarried but lived under one roof with José Baldovino, driller, with whom she procreated, giving birth to David and María, five and eight years old respectively. The document also notes that Brígida would have stated that the fire that killed José "was started accidentally, as is public knowledge and a well-known fact," and that she cannot sign as she is illiterate.

Crescencia Flores, according to the record, was "dishonored" when she was a minor. This is in the statement of Rafael Salinas, who attests that he knew miner Luis Garfias very well and can confirm that Luis and Crescencia Flores lived together out of wedlock and that "she would have been his wife since they were officially ordered by the authorities to be married at Zerezo registry office in light of the fact that Garfias dishonored her, but since they were unaware that Flores was a minor they were unable to arrange the marriage and out of ignorance lived together out of wedlock."

Josefa Ramírez, born in Hacienda del Salitre, Guanajuato, states that she cannot prove she is the mother of pick miner Francisco Velásquez, who died in the El Bordo fire, but that she has brought with her Señor Tomás Ayala and Señor Pedro Bolaños for this purpose; these witnesses attest to the fact that they knew Francisco Velásquez and knew Josefa Ramírez as his mother and affirm that at the time of his death he lived with her, and do not sign as they don't know how to write.

Señores Catarino Rodríguez and Modesto Herrera brought citizen Diego Noble before the auxiliary judge of San Guillermo, Hidalgo, to certify that they had known Fidencio Ortega — who died "accidentally" in the El Bordo mine — for over ten years, that he had spent his whole life with his mother, Señora Isidra Alvarado, that he was from the town of El Doctor, Querétaro, was a bachelor, a pick miner and twenty years old. Their statement is signed.

María Luz Barrios of Tlalpujahua ("she knows not which state"), single, twenty-eight years old, employed "in the domestic labors of her gender . . . with a stand where she [sold] food, or refreshment," came to identify Juan Barrios, El Bordo fireman. Neighbors of María Luz, in turn, came to confirm her relationship to Juan, who had lived with her since she became widowed, and Juan had raised and cared for her daughters Amparo and Vicenta, one of whom was deaf-mute and had a drooping jaw as the result of an operation. Juan earned three pesos fifty centavos a day; they affirm that their testimony is made without malice. There follow twenty signatures. Twenty.

THE EXPERT REPORT

On March 20 the judge ordered Berry to have the mine disinfected on the 21st so that the authorities could go in on the 22nd and inspect it. *Once it had been disinfected* – that was what he ordered, though the crews must have understood him to mean more than that, as they immediately began cleaning and repairs. So the first experts went in after mine administrators had inspected the vestiges of the disaster and after mining crews had begun sweeping up.

The experts found everything to be in perfect order: the eight-inch and one-inch air pipes, in perfect order; the potable water pipe and the firefighting water pipe, in perfect order; the electricity cables, in perfect order; a ladder inside the mine, in perfect order. They found all of this after having descended hundreds of meters and traversed "narrow wooden ladders placed firmly over chasms," as they felt obliged to note, because it's one thing for miners to do it every day and another for educated men to do so.

The report notes that on one of the levels inspected, 142, everything was in perfect order and people were already cleaning and disinfecting the mine. They also came across crews of people cleaning on 207, where the station was found to have literally everything in working order – everything. It's all catalogued: storeroom, ladders, piping, chute, control panel, and trapdoors to the levels below where the track lines ran; even the telephone (the one that didn't work when the survivors were desperately trying to communicate with the surface; Félix García specifically said that they tried to use that phone and it did not work). Incidentally, on this level, which is the one where the survivors were found, not only were there people already engaged in clean-up, but even before that and before the inspectors arrived, miners had already been sent to work the seam.

Only then did the official inspector, José Aurelio García, commissioner of the Ministry of Industry, Commerce and Labor, enter the mine with the aim of producing the definitive report, the penultimate link in the chain of events that erected the official silence around the El Bordo fire. A whole series of authorities had laid the ground; they and he had both been tasked with translating the vestiges of the fire into a language suited to the construction of an innocuous version of it.

The physicians, the engineers, and the photographer are all translators who read the stones and corpses, giving the multiplicity of the physical world a confined set of meanings useful for the judge in his interpretation: signs, causes, evidence of how events unfolded. In the absence of definitive proof, the "knowledge" provided by these individuals – that the miners were all dead just a few hours after the fire began, for example, or that the corpses trapped hundreds of meters below ground had putrefied within forty-eight hours, despite the fact that not one of them had been seen – was enough to influence the opinions of the other authorities. All of this information, this "knowledge," was accepted without question.

The court clerks are translators of voice: they listen to citizens unqualified to enter into dialogue with the law and transform their voices – unique, unpolished – into a neutral universal voice that fits the legal codes used in proceedings.

The judges and magistrates are the ones who open and close the circle: they trigger the actions whose results are recorded in the report, which they will ultimately interpret before issuing the final, definitive speech act. The "civil judge" (emphasis always on his status as member of the republic) is, in the first instance, a reader. He interprets the text he's been given, which already includes a recommendation. But he is not the author of the text, and therefore not the only one responsible for the decision made.

The mayor is a figurehead: he turns up at inspections, appears in court, grants his signature, but he orders nothing, determines nothing, gives no opinions – or if he does, nobody takes them into consideration. To call him a figurehead, however, is not a mere insult: this decorative figure, who forms part of the ceremony, helps achieve the goal of legitimizing the process; he lends formality and institutional weight. His translation renders the banal significant, renders the informal official.

These translating authorities appear as neutral, as rational, as people with no fears or biases, and when their bias comes to light it seems as if they were simply employing common sense, as if they were pointing out something quite evident: that none of the miners are still alive, or that one of them is guilty of starting the fire, for instance.

So when the expert, Inspector Aurelio García, finally made his descent into the mine, he did so with guidelines from the district judge asking him to investigate eleven things:

1. What the source of the fire was or may have been;
2. If the source cannot be determined, what causes can be discounted, that is, determined *not* to have been the source of the fire;
3. Whether the mine has an adequate telephone system able to raise the cry of alarm in case of catastrophe, both from the surface to all underground work zones and between all underground work areas;
4. Whether monitoring of all underground mine sectors is sufficient to control and stop outbreaks of fire;
5. What fire safety measures the mine has, that is, deterrent measures in place to prevent it;

6. Whether all levels of the mine have access to the Santa Ana mine and the Sacramento shaft;
7. Whether cage cables were in good working order prior to the fire;
8. Whether the cages offer the necessary safety for workers' entry and exit;
9. What cage capacity is;
10. What materials are used to shore up the mine shafts;
11. Whether or not the Company operating this mine meets each and every one of the clauses of the Safety and Policing Regulations for Mineworks.

And he should do this to "the best of his knowledge and understanding in his profession" without solely limiting himself to the questions.

And these are the instructions that the judge did NOT put forward to the inspector:

He did not instruct him to inspect *before* cleaning crews went in.

He did not instruct him to confront administrators about the contradictions between what the survivors said in their statements and what the administrators claimed.

He did not instruct him to find out why there was so great a discrepancy in the numbers of dead miners given.

He did not instruct him to try to find out how many other people could have been alive when the shafts were sealed.

He did not instruct him to determine whether the administrators had been criminally negligent in ordering the shafts sealed while there were people still alive inside, as, indeed, there were.

On August 18, nearly five months after beginning his inspection, Irineo Quintero, agent of the public prosecutor's office, in view of the judgment issued by the officially appointed expert, Inspector Engineer José Aurelio García, requested that the case be dismissed, since as per the report it was impossible to determine the cause of the fire and there was, therefore, no crime to prosecute nor any person who might be held criminally responsible. The report contains not the slightest suggestion that someone could be held accountable for the deaths caused by the sealing of the shafts while miners were still alive inside, but it does explicitly back the theory that the fire may have been caused by a worker.

Six days later, the judge granted the dismissal and ordered the case to be closed.

This is what Inspector García saw:

First, the number of people who worked at El Bordo and the way they were assigned. "In the El Bordo mine, an average of 800 men work every twenty-four hours, and of these 530 do so inside the mine. To organize labor, the mine is divided into three sectors, A, B, and C; the first is comprised of the surface to level 305; the second, levels 305 to 415; and the third, everything below 415. Each sector is under the supervision of two muckers, one deputy foreman, one captain, and one foreman, and the entire mine is under the direction of the superintendent who receives his instructions from the director general."

Later he states, with regard to workers' salaries: "There are three shifts in the mine, each corresponding to an eight-hour workday. Jobs are for the most part done by contract and, to a lesser extent, by day laborers who receive a minimum wage of $1.80 (one peso eighty centavos) per day and a maximum wage of $6.00 (six pesos) per day and an average of $2.60 (two pesos sixty centavos). For piecework, laborers receive higher sums than those noted." Following this, he felt it necessary to add that "for as long as the Company has been in operation, that is, from 1918 to the present, there has been no record of strikes."

The inspector also confirmed that the mining engineer's degree was valid, that the logbook kept a record of the workers going in every day and checked them off on the way out to note their departure, that no workers were under the age of twelve, that the department storerooms were equipped with alcohol, disinfectant, gauze, cotton, and provisions for the immediate treatment of wounds, and that on the surface there was a first aid room, with a first aid kit more complete than those in the storerooms.

García recounts that when he entered the mine, the El Bordo shaft had already been completely cleaned and the La Luz and the Sacramento were in the process of being cleaned. He saw no conflict between this fact and his subsequent observations, in which he unreservedly commends the state of the mine. He notes that the ladders and the climbing shafts in which they are located meet the necessary safety requirements, that the shafts are surrounded by rails and grates to impede accidents, that the whim-rooms, shaft mouths and all of the stations have control panels for the operation of extraction machinery, and that it is clearly stipulated that only the station supervisors and a man who rides the cages constantly are in charge of sending signals. In light of all of this, he notes, it is clear that the mine meets the provisions of the Safety and Policing Regulations for Mineworks.

In fact, more than meet minimum requirements, the inspector found that the Company went beyond what was compulsory, as seen in this paragraph, which exemplifies the goodwill he displays toward the bosses:

The Company that currently runs the El Bordo mine shows concern for all that improves the health and safety of their workers; as such they are organizing rescue units by outfitting them with the necessary equipment such as masks or helmets supplied with oxygen, electric lamps, etc., so they can enter areas where breathing is impossible; they are also ensuring systematic practice

drills for the use of said equipment and the treatment of
the wounded and injured in order to be ready should an
accident occur; the Company has undertaken a campaign
to prevent accidents, and has issued provisions to limit
them, including one that restricts workers' consumption
of pulque; with this provision they have succeeded not
only in decreasing the number of accidents but also in
improving relations between superiors and subordinates,
as there are no longer threats of strike and relatively few
disagreements; inside the mine, care is always taken to
ensure the utmost cleanliness, for which purpose on all
levels there are buckets of lime that serve as toilets which
as soon as they are full are taken out to be emptied, and
the levels with most traffic are sprayed daily with water
to keep dust down; preparatory and exploratory work,
and some production work, is done with mechanical
drills, which clearly reduces the physical effort required
of workers, and, as in the mine, care is taken to use water
with the drills in order to impede the formation of dust
so there is no danger to the health of those operating
them; outside the mine there are hot and cold showers
as well as English-style toilets that can be used free of
charge by workers and employees.

It is worth highlighting some of the things the inspector
finds impressive: that the miners can use the bathroom
without having to pay; that state-of-the-art technology
allows the miners not to risk accidents or hazards to
their health (he honestly said that); that by limiting the

consumption of pulque there are few disagreements between superiors and subordinates and have been no strikes, which is a logical conclusion if one has read the previous information carefully: with owners so concerned about their workers, what possible cause could there be for discord if not drunkenness? Dissent, or worse yet, rebellion, could be explained only if the workers were intoxicated; it couldn't possibly be a lucid expression, the pursuit of justice.

The inspector, quite taken, does not limit himself to the conditions in the mine after it had been cleaned but goes on to record in his report a number of measures that the owners said they were *planning* to undertake, including: placing an 8000 m^3/m ventilation fan at the mouth of the Sacramento shaft for the extraction of foul air; installing compressed-air nozzles to spray mist and distribute it more uniformly throughout the pit props by taking advantage of the airflow; elongating level 365 so that the El Bordo would connect to the Dinamita mine; beginning construction on a manway between level 415 and the surface in order to have one more exit in case of emergency. The report includes an appendix detailing all of these good intentions expressed by the Company.

Eventually, the inspector gives his report on "the claim."

According to Expert Inspector García's observations, the fire broke out at six in the morning (not "around," or "close to" or "possibly" but "at six," he asserts, with a certainty that leaves readers hopeful that from this point on everything will be equally clear and specific), between levels 415 and 365, "possibly very near the 392." He justifies this imprecision, stating only that it is impossible to determine the exact spot where the fire began (despite the fact that, *seeing no inconsistency whatsoever*, he does claim to know the exact hour). He indicates that the deputy foremen were the first to perceive the fire, and that they and the muckers were the ones who raised the cry of alarm and began evacuation efforts. He notes that the last to get out were deputy foremen Edmundo Olascoaga and José Linares, but that Antonio López de Nava and eighty-seven other miners, who at this point he doesn't name, were unable to do so.

According to García's report, it was the medical, civic, and business authorities together who made the decision to close the mine: Doctors Asiáin and Espínola claimed it was "unquestionable" that if any miners were still inside the mine they were already dead, asphyxiated by the carbon gas, since no one could survive even five minutes in air so heavy with it. This bears repeating: the doctors proclaimed the deaths of all those still in the mine without having examined a single one of them. Therefore, states the report, the administrators, in the presence of the district judge and the mayor, ordered access to the Santa Ana to be sealed at twelve o'clock, and sealed the El Bordo and La Luz shafts at three o'clock in the afternoon.

Inspector García took the authorities' word without hesitation, despite the fact that in the dossier itself there are contradictions between their statements. The first to justify sealing the shafts was Berry, who, just a few hours after the fire began, made the call because, as he claimed: 1) the fire had already been extinguished and all that remained to be done was ensure that it was completely extinguished; and 2) it was necessary in order to recover the bodies, which could number no more than ten; because 3) he knew that "all the people were already out."

Let's examine the testimony verbatim. At twelve o'clock on March 10, a statement was taken from J. F. Berry in which, according to the report, he asserts:

the fire in the El Bordo shaft is already out and work will continue with a view to completely extinguishing the fire, for which purpose the El Bordo shaft will be hermetically sealed and then immediately thereafter so will the La Luz, which belongs to the same mine and through which smoke is at present escaping, La Luz being a shaft that cannot catch fire because it has no woodwork and is built entirely of masonry and steel beams; that later, once the smoke is gone, people will begin their descent through that shaft, with a view to seeing the results of the fire and what repairs will be necessary in the depths of the mine, as well as recovering any bodies that might be inside; that until then [Berry] can only presume the existence of exactly ten bodies and does not believe there to be any more, because at the time the fire began the

majority of people had already gotten out, since [Berry]
knows that the last deputy foreman underground is
one by the name of Linares, who will also give a statement, and who says he got all of his people out; but that
[Berry] will, in any case, fulfill his duty by reporting the
exact number of dead, whatever that might be, once this
number is known.

Of course, if you continue to read the report, it's easy to
verify: 1) that the fire was not out (and that they knew
this that very day); 2) that there were more than ten dead
(which they also learned the same day, or at least learned
that there were more than ten men still in the mine); and
3) that there are no witnesses to back up Berry's assertion
that all the workers got out; in fact, on the next page is
the statement given by José Linares, a statement that, I
repeat, comes on *the very next page after Berry's claim*,
in which he "asserts that from the 525 he called the workers on the 415 by telephone and they did not respond the
several times he called, and therefore he doesn't know
what happened to those men, but there was still time
to get out."

This witness states three things: that he attempted
to notify people of the fire; that he *does not know* what
happened to the men; and that there was still time to get
them out. These are matters on which he is a qualified
witness, but Berry's statement, which no one questions
and which rests on the supposed testimony of this witness,

credits him with saying something different; nevertheless, Berry's is the statement used to support a decision which contradicts Linares's actual testimony. Regardless, none of the claims put forward by the superintendent to justify sealing the shafts while there were still people in the mine alive stands up. All of the certainties and assumptions on which his decision was based were wrong, or invented, and yet no action was taken to investigate the contradictions regardless of the fact that they are recorded *on the next page*; these are not discoveries made a posteriori, not contradictions that cropped up long after the fact, but on the very same day or one day later at most.

The final number of dead that Inspector García offers is seventy-seven, a number he asserts with satisfaction, as this way it tallies perfectly with the number recorded in the logbook: adding the seven survivors, seventy-seven dead and three individuals who left the mine without ticking their names off yields eighty-seven, "which is how many were missing according to the logbook, once it had been rectified." *Once it had been rectified.* The logbook originally said something different, but it was "rectified." The seventy-seven corpses were autopsied, and the doctors invariably concluded cause of death as asphyxiation. Although they had all of the names of the dead, seven of the bodies were never identified. The report notes perfunctorily that the Company made the decision, authorized by the state government, to bury them all on a plot of land on mine property in order to keep the bodies from being carried in procession through town, "with the aim of preventing an epidemic brought on by so many corpses passing through the city of Pachuca." There is no record of what the family members felt at not being allowed to bury their loved ones where they wished. It's a final gesture on the part of the Company to make clear what had previously been carried out via worker exploitation: that all of those bodies, living or dead, were Company property.

Inspector García groups the names* of the identified bodies by job and wage in pesos: "Antonio López de Nava, deputy foreman, $6.00; Valentín Magos, Pedro Estrada, Teodoro Landero, and Carmen Gutiérres, contract workers, $3.50; Marciano Trejo and Juan Sosa, muckers, $3.00; Cruz Vega, Jesús Acosta, Francisco Lara, Vicente Guillén, José Patricio and Eulalio Valerio, drillers, $2.40; Juan Barrios, fireman, $2.50; Luis Garfias, cager, $2.00; Francisco Magos, assistant driller, $1.80; Domingo Hernández, Erasto Chávez, Aristeo Reyes, Francisco Ortiz, Marcos López, Francisco Cortés, Esteban Martínez, Donaciano López, José Trejo, Toribio Ruiz, Guadalupe Pérez, Vicente Peña, José Valdovinos, Hilario Cruz, Jesús Pagola, Amado Pagola, Luis González, Zenobio López, Genaro Nava, Agustín González, Fidencio Ortega, José Terrez (elsewhere

---

* The report makes numerous mistakes with the spellings of surnames, as do many of the official documents related to the case. I have transcribed these names exactly as they appear.

identified as Torres), Miguel Álvarez, Ángel Montaño, Benjamín Morales, Amador Torres, Simón Arrasola, José Jiménez, Félix Delgado, Juan Fernández, Jesús Martínez, Bartolo Corona, Leobardo González, José Montiel, Fidel Guerrero, Melquíades Ortiz, Bartolo Lozano, Isaac Villanueva, Pedro García, Juan Bolaños, Aurelio Juárez, José Mendiola, Margarito Torres, Cleofás Molinero, Cesáreo Bolaños, Bonifacio Romero, Toribio Velásquez, Francisco Velásquez, Guadalupe Lozada, Anastasio Luna, Antonio Molinero, Bartolo Corona, Tomás García, Gilberto Banda and Miguel Martínez, day laborers, $1.80."

Having named the dead he could name, Inspector García recounts what he found during his inspection after the fire (and after Company workers had gone through cleaning up). On level 207 the timbering was "fully intact," the storeroom and station telephone had suffered no damage (no damage and yet was unusable, as we saw), the ventilation doors were in good condition, and the dynamite stored in a crosscut to the west of the El Bordo shaft showed no sign of anything abnormal. He also mentions that he inspected the spot where the survivors were and the place on this level where they found four dead bodies – presumably where those who went in search of carbide fell – though he gives no more details in this respect.

He does however give details about the fire's reach, saying that it was limited to the El Bordo shaft, "extending from level 465 to 5 marks (8.75 m) above level 305, i.e. a distance of 168.75 meters, and of that length, 85 meters (from level 415 to 330) were left with no timbering or piping or other fixtures, as they were completely destroyed, while in the remaining meters the timbering was scorched but did not fall and the piping and fixtures were somewhat damaged," and that it most likely began on level 392, "since this is just below the center of the destruction and the outer limits of the fire," but that he found no indication of what had caused the fire. And, of course, he notes that the mine's safety standards were satisfactory.

Thereafter, Inspector García discards the possible causes of the fire.

It could not have been a natural cause "because in this mine there was no coal dust susceptible to overheating and, by extension, producing spontaneous combustion that could then ignite the wooden timbering."

It could not have been caused by gas or airborne dust that would ignite on contact with an open-flame lamp because El Bordo was not a coal mine, and that only happens in coal mines.

It could not have been caused by a short circuit in the electrical cables descending into the mine because that would have been detected on the control panels (which, as we know, were functioning perfectly, like everything else) and would have automatically shut off the electrical current; he states that if the Limit-Overload-Relay security apparatus had not worked the short-circuit would have jammed the transformers and caused a discharge of oil, and none of that had occurred.

It could not have been any of the most common causes of mining accidents such as, the inspector goes on to list, a lamp accidentally left on the timbering, a cooking fire, or a lit cigarette or match, since timbering takes a long time to catch fire due to its thickness and the fact that it's damp with steam released in the shaft's airflow, and the fire would have been quickly detected from all the smoke it would have produced.

Therefore, as Inspector García sees it, only one possible cause of fire remains, and with it he concludes his work: a worker was to blame. He couldn't dare to venture that it was arson, because he has no proof of that; nevertheless, although he also has no evidence of where the fire began, he asserts that due to the speed with which it spread, it must have been started "by the igniting of highly flammable substances, such as petroleum or gasoline," and most likely some fireman or mechanic was transporting it to clean the machinery and accidentally spilled a container of fuel on the wood in the station or the shaft. He doesn't specify where. Nor exactly how. But he can say exactly when. And he can venture to guess which kind of who.

In his conclusions the inspector endorses this theory and discards the others, reiterates that the mine has good safety standards and that the Company met the Safety and Policing Regulations for Mineworks. He acknowledges only two criticisms of the Company. The first is that they did not notify the Ministry of Industry, Commerce and Labor of the fire. The second – a brief, tangential criticism that has occupied me, though I still feel unable to discern its significance entirely – is that a powder magazine the Company owns in another part of the city, close to Hacienda de Cuesco, does not meet safety regulations, as the explosives are not sufficiently isolated from public streets, nor does it have the means to put out a possible fire. So, he does concede the possibility that due to the negligent management of explosives on the Company's part there could at some point be a fire, and yet he's not talking about El Bordo but another place where they store explosives. He includes this in the report although he's talking about a different fire, a hypothetical one, in a warehouse on the other side of town.

I am tempted to say that this is some sort of coded message, that this officer of the law actually wants to indicate that the owners are responsible for the fire, for some fire, albeit one that never happened, but he can't say it. (This is akin to what Borges recounts in "Theme of the Traitor and the Hero," where a man named Ryan, who is writing the biography of his great-grandfather, the Irish nationalist Kilpatrick, discovers that the man was actually a traitor. To keep from imperiling the movement, Kilpatrick's companions staged a martyr's death for him and scripted it, borrowing from Shakespeare for tragic effect. But it turned out that references to the bard were unnecessary: "In Nolan's work, the passages imitating Shakespeare are the *least* dramatic; Ryan suspects that the author slipped them in so that someone, in the future, would uncover the truth.") And yet this is sheer speculation. What's certain is that the inspector fulfilled his directive: he looked at some things, neglected to look at others, and unreservedly exculpated the mine owners and administrators.

THE GRAVE

The grave had been readied even before there were any bodies to put in it. In the case file is a letter from the administrator of Pachuca Civil Hospital to the district judge, dated March 12, in which he expresses concern, anticipating that the corpses will be sent to his hospital. At this point it's been approximately forty-eight hours – depending on which version you believe – since the start of the fire, but the hospital administrator is sure that the bodies "must already be in a complete state of putrefaction, and the transporting of them, as well as their stay at this Establishment, given the current circumstances with the influenza epidemic, could occasion infection and increased illness," which is why he requests that the judge remove the provision to perform autopsies, "given that the cause of death is known for all of them." In actual fact, at this point there were men inside the mine who weren't dead.

In response, the Civil Registry judge sent an official letter on behalf of the district judge responding to the note, informing the administrator of the request made by J. F. Berry, superintendent of the company, to bury the dead in an empty lot "adjacent to the graveyard in the town of Zerezo, located behind the aforementioned mine, with the aim of avoiding difficulties for the relatives as well as hazards to public health." The first judge who authorizes the other judge to communicate with the superintendent indicates, in turn, that he authorizes the interment authorized by the civil governor. The town's name, by the way, is in fact Cerezo, but none of the authorities communicating the order seems concerned with correctly spelling the name of the place where they would abandon the victims.

That same day, March 12, *El Universal* publishes the testimonies of anonymous informants claiming that people have been stealing metal from the mine for some time, and at the Company's efforts to discover who it was, the "bandits" probably set it on fire. The reporter says that this "exquisite detail" was denied by no one and confirms the belief held by the "owner of the mine" that it may have been arson. The following day, the same paper recounts the decision to prevent the bodies from entering the city and states that the judge approved the proposal in order to keep Pachuca residents from being subjected to a "sorrowful shock" on seeing the funeral cortege go by. Three days later he supplemented this information, assuring readers that the land acquired by the Company where they were going to bury the dead (whose numbers no one knew and who at the time were not in fact even known to be dead) would be walled, and that there they would erect a monument in memory of the victims of the fire. Neither of those things happened.

I've seen a photo that says, on the back, "Funeral procession for the miners killed at El Bordo," but there is nothing in it to indicate that that's actually what it is. I don't recognize the street as being in Pachuca, although it could have changed (and what made it recognizable is no longer there). And the procession is a motorcade, with lots of cars, at a time when there were very few cars in Pachuca, especially among miners. I suppose it's not out of the question that, contrary to all of the documents and *crónicas* and oral memories, there could have been a procession, but I think it's more likely that someone attributed the photo to a nonexistent procession in the belief that it was the decent thing to do: treat the dead like human beings who deserve a send-off from their loved ones, not like trash to be hidden at the earliest convenience.

There was a certain urgency to make the numbers tally as quickly as possible. Numbers always give the impression that what's being said is somehow solid. That's why the file states that once the last bodies were recovered, on March 20, the only thing left to do was add and subtract in order to determine how many people were still inside the mine on the day of the fire. By this operation, they had brought out seventy-seven bodies at the time, and since the logbook stated that there were eighty-four people, the seven survivors completed the list; later it was claimed that the logbook actually recorded eighty-seven people, three of whom had left the mine without checking off their names. And yet, with no explanation of the discrepancy, the case file states that there were eighty-eight people trapped in the mine ("Antonio López de Nava . . . and eighty-seven workers").

After the first extraction of bodies, the authorities methodically began to catalogue them. They conducted autopsies as the remains were recovered, and attempted to identify who they belonged to. If a determination was not made in twenty-four hours, the body was buried anonymously on the plot the Company had prepared. But the authorities began describing them as ex-humans the moment they started being pulled out: "All of the corpses were completely disfigured, many of them charred and most completely black, swollen, scorched to the degree that the majority had lost all human form, the skin disintegrated or peeled off like a glove from a hand. Many wore a handkerchief over the nose and had a tongue sticking out and some of their limbs broken off."

An initial list in the case file includes the names of seventy-seven bodies that were identified and eight that were unidentified. The vast majority of death certificates register almost exactly the same findings for each body and follow the same format: "No sign of traumatic injury, relatively advanced putrefaction. The viscera show all pathoanatomical signs of gas asphyxiation, said condition being cause of death."

There are exceptions, however, including those of Pedro García and J. Jesús Martínez, who each died twice, once of cranial fracture and a second time by asphyxiation. Pedro García's certificate states: "The cause of death in the present case was skull fracture as well as the previously described asphyxia." And J. Jesús Martínez's certificate reads: "The skull fracture is of the sort that endangers life and in the present case was, along with asphyxia, the cause of death."

Another body was logged as "Unknown or Francisco Velásquez" and then, assuming it was the latter, lists his personal details: native of Hacienda El Salitre, in Guanajuato, single, fourteen years of age, day laborer, son of Tomás Velásquez and Josefa Ramírez.

Another exception is José Cruz Vera, whose wound is described in detail as being "situated in the frontal region, to the right of the midline, front to back, approximately ten centimeters in length, which penetrated the scalp entirely without fracturing the skull." But there is no additional explanation as to what might have occasioned the injury.

And J. Jesús Acosta had a wound described as a "contusion, located in the region of the mesogastrium, approximately ten centimeters, along which several loops of the small bowel are herniated."

Despite the celerity with which they began to shelve the case, voices of dissent, pain, and even rage do exist on record:

For example, on March 14, *Excélsior* reports that the Socialist Workers' Party and kindred organizations called for eight days of mourning and requested that, as a mark of respect, all concerts be postponed.

And one of the few traces of the mourning that people were, indeed, going through can be seen in the mention of a pamphlet written by Deputy Alberto Vargas, in which he noted what, he said, was a conviction shared throughout the city, and one that the case file very carefully avoided suggesting: that the Company was responsible for the fire, the deaths, and the way the dead were treated. As a result of this pamphlet, the judge called Deputy Vargas to testify, and he turned up at court prepared for a fight. He declared that he stood by what he'd said, that he'd said as much in articles in *El Gladiador* newspaper and a speech to the state legislature, that as deputy he could not be tried for his opinions, and that he'd committed no crime. The judge replied that he was not "yet" being accused of anything and had been called in not to give opinions but as a witness, and as such should tell them what he knew, if indeed he knew anything. Deputy Vargas then stated that he had no proof as to whether the fire had been intentional or not, that he was only expressing the voice of the people, which he'd heard "entering cantinas and mingling at several social gatherings," but that he was not prepared to name the people accusing the Santa Gertrudis Company because he didn't know them all and because the whole town was saying this. The file notes, on the same page, that the court respects the freedom of the press and that the deputy was only called to testify because he'd made his opinions known.

In addition to this, on March 13, less than seventy-six hours after the start of the fire and before anyone had a clue what had happened, Puebla de Zaragoza's seventh-district magistrate, Emilio Cruz, upon hearing of the accident, warned the district judge: "with great displeasure that, because accidents of the type . . . continue to occur with such frequency in your jurisdiction, and as it is not at all unusual for these accidents to stem from repeated oversights and lack of precaution and the absence of punishment for those found guilty, I recommend that in this and other cases that may occur you proceed with the great urgency and efficacy due." Lack of punishment with regard to *past* events, he meant.

So, in theory it would seem that the magistrate is a kind of hero willing to swim against the tide, that he is determined to tell it like it is, denounce injustice and fight for the truth; it would seem that his voice was simply not heard. But in fact, this is the moment of anagnorisis, when one actor recognizes another, exposes his history and his intentions and proclaims that he sees all. The magistrate expresses his feelings on the matter and anticipates the results of the investigation ("the absence of punishment for those found guilty"), but does not continue to intervene or otherwise ensure the proceedings are indeed given the "great urgency and efficacy due." His work as an augur is done: he's established that if he can be sure of one thing, it's that the law sees all, and that he's not fooled with respect to the way its institutions and agents function on a daily basis; if his reaction to this is only an exhortation that has no consequences, that means the reality he described was seen as acceptable. The magistrate is not voiceless, it's simply that his voice is used not so much to be obeyed as it is to underscore, by way of contrast, a greater good: the perseverance of institutions regardless of their relationship to justice. And in the end, considering how precisely his auguries came to pass, it's fair to say that the procedure truly was conducted with efficacy due.

THE MANY DAYS
THAT FOLLOWED

On March 15 a convoy of day-trippers passed through El Bordo without stopping. *Excélsior* reported that they had lunch in nearby El Hiloche, cast racing pigeons into the sky, and played baseball. The paper also reported that on March 21 an automobile rally passed through the outskirts of Pachuca, with over thirty cars taking part. "It was sponsored by Auto Club México. There were no accidents; distinguished families attended." The piece included photos of the drivers, their wives and children posing by the cars or enjoying a picnic like people who have no idea they're being photographed.

On March 31 a piece in *El Universal* announced that there would soon be jobs for up to 10,000 people in Pachuca, with wages ranging from $2 to $12 pesos per day, thanks to initiatives of mining companies based in the state of Hidalgo. "Their skills will be put to use as builders, with wages from $2 to $3.50; carpenters, $2.50 to $3.50; mechanics, $3.50 to $12 per day; and electricians, from $3.50 to $12 per day."

"Normality," good fortune, and the promise of a bright

future were already being promoted while the living were still trapped underground with the dead, while inquiries into what happened were still going on. There was a need to close the file on this story, and to do so on metal as well as paper, as we'll see.

On September 16, the object I mentioned on the first page of this book was unveiled. The object is a plaque, on a gazebo, in a park. The park is Parque Hidalgo, located one kilometer southwest of the city center and 300 meters northeast of Pachuca Civil Hospital. In other words, it's in between the two places where a funeral procession carrying the miners' bodies would necessarily have passed, had any public display of mourning been permitted.

The gazebo's base measures 10.64 m by 11.64 m and is raised 1.45 m off the ground. It has cast-iron handrails, which stop at a five-step staircase made of stone. The handrails, as well as some gargoyle-shaped lamps, were added after the gazebo's inauguration. The longer sides feature cast-iron arcades of four columns each, approximately five meters high. The plaque is on the lower part of the gazebo's north wall. It measures 23 cm by 63.5 cm and is raised 64 cm off the ground; it's made of bronze, and the sans serif letters embossed upon it measure approximately 4 cm by 2.4 cm each.

The plaque reads:

A · G I F T · F R O M · T H E
A M E R I C A N · C O M M U N I T Y · T O
T H E · S T A T E · G O V E R N M E N T
S E P T E M B E R · 1 6 · 1 9 2 0

There are other monuments in the park as well: a bust of Josefa Ortiz de Domínguez; a bust of Miguel Hidalgo y Costilla; a bust of Governor Carlos Ramírez Guerrero (state governor from 1963–1969); a bust of Prof. Francisco Noble erected by his students; a plaque expressing gratitude to President Luis Echeverría Álvarez and Governor Manuel Sánchez Vite for the restoration of the park, cafeteria and rides; a bust of Vicente Aguirre del Castillo (governor, 1945–1951); and in one corner, a horrendous "peace dove" that is literally made of rifles and pistols, unveiled under the mayorship of Eleazar García (2012–2016). There is also, some twenty meters northeast of the gazebo, a fountain with a plaque reading:

MONUMENT DONATED BY THE SPANISH COMMUNITY TO THE CITY OF PACHUCA, IN THE YEAR 1910, ON THE OCCASION OF THE 100TH ANNIVERSARY OF MEXICAN INDEPENDENCE.

And a floral clock.

Half of the monuments are in honor of governors and liberators of the state and nation, and the gazebo donated by the "American community" names the state government as the recipient of their gift – a gift on the occasion of some independence day celebration or other, a regular old Cry of Independence anniversary, *not* the centenary, like the fountain given by the Spanish.

The plaque, without so much as mentioning it, is talking about the El Bordo mine fire. What makes me say this? I might speculate that the explicit message on the plaque is an acknowledgment of the complicity shown by Governor Flores, who, according to the press, was listening to classical music as the drama unfolded and never even so much as came to see what was going on. And yet I think the monument says what it says not only through what it clearly states but also through the specific tension in which its letters were inscribed. Let me explain.

What is the act of giving? An undertaking of generosity that defines both giver and recipient. This gift is a gazebo in the middle of a park: a public space, potentially an agora. But the power of the object given is restricted. What happens with it must be controlled and what happens around it must be sanctioned by the clearly designated recipient – and the designated recipient of this gift is clearly the "state government." This was not because people were waiting for a space to organize and reignite the revolution, or to prevent the mere sight of the gazebo from triggering a wave of "divine violence," but the act of naming the recipient of a public space does specify the relationship between donor and user of the space. The gesture excludes the local populace from a public act, only allowing it if mediated by the government. And that exclusion, memorialized in the monument, is also the tension of the text as it's inscribed. Why was the monument necessary and why doesn't it mention the people who will use it?

The "American community" could have chosen any year to commemorate Mexican independence: the centenary had been celebrated ten years earlier and there seems to have been no reason to celebrate it again ten years on. The subtext, however, is not how timely it is historically but how necessary politically. This is the only monument in the city that the self-described "American community" publicly dedicated, and they did so just six months after at least eighty-seven people were trapped in a burning metal mine by order of its administrators – the most powerful members of said "community."

This was the most conspicuous interaction between the "American community" and the "Pachuca community" up to the time when the pavilion was inaugurated, which is why it's impossible not to see it as part of the same story; it's an unsurprising irony that the text in which this tension is inscribed is on *a metal plaque.*

The plaque in Parque Hidalgo does not offer a distorted version of the facts; rather, it's a dodge, an evasive move: it affirms, in broad daylight, just how nonessential the whole story is, and places the subjects who might be reproached for their part in the tragedy out of harm's way, far from the fire. Those subjects are allocated a space of generosity: the "American community" is a *giving* community. The inscription may be the one gaffe in the gesture, the sign that it still wasn't possible to address the "Pachuca community" directly, and that the "state government" was tasked with ensuring that use of the space legitimized the silence to which it alludes.

That silence took multiple forms in the months of normalization that followed, some of them quite active. A press release in *El Universal*, for instance, published five days after the gazebo was inaugurated, talks of "Bolshevik elements" and their activism among the Pachuca miners, who reject it because their working conditions are unbeatable. It merits looking at the entire text:

> Certain Bolshevik elements have tried to implant their ideas, winning over the labor leaders working in the mines; but, no doubt due to the comfortable conditions miners enjoy throughout the region, the propagandists were left "hamstrung." Soviet ideas are not to our workers' liking and, with respect to this matter, the mining companies coexist in perfect harmony with their workers. Happily, in the Hidalgo mining district, there have been no reports of work stoppages or strikes. Everyone earns very high wages, which allow them to live comfortably, and on their days of rest most employees and workers engage in sport. There are close to twenty baseball and football teams in Pachuca and Real del Monte, and everybody finds a form of entertainment.

Happiness, perfect harmony, entertainment. High wages, comfortable lives, days of rest. They're talking about the same lucky miners whose bosses, a few months earlier, had decided to bury dozens of their workmates alive, and about their families, who were forced to undergo humiliating interrogations in order to obtain compensation that might help them endure poverty. It matters little if the piece is, as it would seem, nothing but a Company-sponsored insert. It's a propagandistic tract that constructs a vision of the mine as a place of harmony and stresses the generosity of its US administrators; and more than that (regardless of who penned it and for the benefit of whom), the text addresses the reader who is part of this social order as someone who should feel satisfied, the same way one might cheer up a hospital patient who's broken all of their bones by saying, "You look great! So lucky you weren't decapitated!"

Later that year, it snowed. It wasn't something that happened regularly, but nor was it the first time that snow had fallen in the mining region. In fact, until recently, it snowed every five or ten years in Real del Monte, the other town in the Pachuca mining district. Snowfalls lasted a few hours, perhaps just enough to dust the ground lightly. That's what it must have done in 1920. A few kilometers away, between Pachuca and Real, snow probably also covered the mass grave where those killed in the El Bordo fire were buried.

But as we've seen, there was no monument or plaque for them; their stories and history survive in the oral memories of the miners' families, the *crónicas* of Félix Castillo ("The Burning of the El Bordo Mine") and José Luis Islas ("Fire at the El Bordo Mine"); and in the Rodolfo Benavides novel *El doble nueve* (The Double Nine), even though officially the case was closed in the many days that followed.

The many days that followed:

In 1923, at the Company's refusal to discuss workplace regulations for the offices, a strike breaks out on January 6; one striker will be murdered. A provisional agreement is reached to discuss regulations on January 16, at the Ministry of the Interior in Mexico City.

In 1930, 600 workers from Real del Monte are fired, protests erupt, and the workers' leader is murdered. At pressure from the state governor, the Company reinstates those who were fired. The same year, the Mine Workers' Alliance is founded in Real del Monte.

In 1934, in Pachuca, the Industrial Union of Mine, Metal and Allied Workers and Employees is founded, later changing its name to the National Union of Mine, Metal, Steel and Allied Workers of the Republic of Mexico. Pachuca and Real del Monte are named sections one and two, for their importance and seniority. The convention leading to the formation of the union is held between April 24 and May 1 and attended by representatives from twenty-seven organizations representing 12,256 miners from the states of Coahuila, Chihuahua, Durango, Guanajuato, Hidalgo, Jalisco, Oaxaca, San Luis Potosí, Sinaloa and Zacatecas.

In 1946, the Dos Carlos Cooperative is created and run by the miners themselves, with the aim of saving their source of employment. This will be a two-year endeavor.

In 1947, as a result of the increased difficulty in finding silver, American investors and administrators abandon mines in the state of Hidalgo.

In 1950, the mines become semi-public property.

In 1965, on May 8, at Purísima Concepción Mine in Real del Monte, a cage transporting thirty miners falls from level 400 to level 550. Twenty-seven are killed.

In 1979, a dissident group called Miners' Liberation splinters from the union.

In 1980, the union calls a strike to improve worker conditions. Women in mining families will play an important role in this strike.

In 1985, on May 24, at 7:30 a.m., in an action that other movements will later copy but which at the time was unheard of, 3,500 miners on the morning shift strip naked to demand safety equipment. Their demands are met the same day. After this successful mobilization, union management starts to suppress internal dissent.

In 1988, as part of a privatization strategy, the Company administration begins mass layoffs.

In 1989 the mines are once again privatized. After this, nearly all are gradually shut down, dismantled, their machinery sold by piece, for the iron. The new owners have not resumed underground exploration and, if anything, are using open-pit extraction.

Something of this story of murder, plunder, and the determination to escape oblivion is palpable when visiting the city. I am from Pachuca and I still don't know exactly what this unspeakable crime – and those before it, and those that followed – did to us, but there's something there. Sometimes it feels like resignation, other times like tolerance, and still others like no one gives a shit; only very rarely does it seem like rage. But whatever it is, it's more than resentment or conformity: despite the story of El Bordo being hidden in a dead file, over all these decades there have been people determined to remember that, contrary to what all those men in fancy suits claimed, down below people were still, are still, alive.

ACKNOWLEDGMENTS

More details from the story of El Bordo remain to be told; and they're there, with the people who inherited the story from their elders. My version is just one attempt to tell it the best I could with the information available to me. I want to thank those who assisted me in my research, as well as the institutions that allowed me to undertake it.

Among those who helped me greatly in Pachuca, I would like to mention Zenón Rosas Franco, who took me for the first time to the exact spot where the El Bordo miners are buried; Félix Castillo García, writer, ex-miner, who lent me his *crónica* of the fire, based on stories he heard while working in the mine; Anselmo Estrada Albuquerque, journalist and ex-miner, who has spent decades documenting life in Hidalgo and has always been willing to answer any questions I had; Enrique Garnica, who accompanied me to study the pavilion in Parque Hidalgo; Pablo Mayans, who told me about the *crónica* written by his grandfather, José Luis Islas; and Moisés Cabrera and Manuel Hurtado, who took me down into the Santa Ana mine.

While conducting this research I worked in several archives: the Mexican General National Archive, the Real del Monte and Pachuca Company Archive, the National Library, the National Newspaper Archives, the UNAM Central Library, and the Bancroft Library at UC Berkeley. I thank the staff at all of these institutions for their help.

I would especially like to thank all those working at the Ministro Manuel Yáñez Ruiz Legal Culture Center in Pachuca, Hidalgo, which houses the Pachuca 1920–1966 case file; the treatment I received from every person there was unfailingly professional and efficient, and they generously allowed me to photograph the four photos in the file. Of course, I thank Heladio Vera, who came to do it.

This book is based on research I undertook while obtaining a PhD in Hispanic Languages and Literatures at UC Berkeley. José Rabasa was my supervisor, and my committee was comprised of Estelle Tarica, Jesús Rodríguez-Velasco and Stanley Brandes. Although this book uses information gathered for and even a few paragraphs from my dissertation, these are two different projects. Not only because for this one I had more information but because they are books whose aims are different. The dissertation, among other things, is an analysis of the materials alluding to and recording the history. This book is aimed at making the story and its protagonists, the Pachuca community, visible.

The following texts helped me concretize information on the 1923 strike, the 1930 protest, the 1934 convention, and the way the union evolved in the 1970s and 1980s:

Nicolás Cárdenas García, *Empresas y trabajadores en la gran minería mexicana, 1900–1929.* México: Secretaría de Gobernación, IEHRM, 1998.

Irma Eugenia Gutiérrez Mejía, "La reconversión industrial en la Compañía Real del Monte y Pachuca. Auge y derrumbe del sindicalismo-democrático en la Sección 1 del SNTMMSRM." Paper given at the Reestructuración Productiva y Reorganización Social Conference. Jalapa, Mexico, October 25–28, 1989.

Juan Luis Sariego, Luis Reygadas, Miguel Ángel Gómez, Javier Farrera, *El Estado y la minería mexicana. Política, trabajo y sociedad durante el siglo XX.* Mexico: FCE / SEMIP, 1988.

Thanks to Tori, my partner, for her love, intelligence, and support every day. To Juan Álvarez for always lending me his critical eye. And thanks to my family, where the history of the mines and the stories of the miners were always present. Of the many memories I have are those of the days when I'd accompany my mother, Irma Eugenia, to the miners' union clinic, on Calle Cuauhtémoc; while she worked, someone from the union would come give me a glass of milk and a pan dulce. To my brother Arturo, who ran off from the time he was a teenager to climb rocks on the old mining routes. And I recall the day after the naked miners' protest, when my Uncle Polo came over with two copies of *La Jornada* and my father Arturo with ten more; *La Jornada* was the only paper in Mexico City that listened to my father when he began notifying the media the night before that in a few hours something extraordinary was going to happen at the mines of Pachuca and Real del Monte.

My brother Tonatiuh was interested from a very early age in what had happened in El Bordo; the oral memory that led me to this story is his.

Dear readers,

As well as relying on bookshop sales, And Other Stories relies on subscriptions from people like you for many of our books, whose stories other publishers often consider too risky to take on.

Our subscribers don't just make the books physically happen. They also help us approach booksellers, because we can demonstrate that our books already have readers and fans. And they give us the security to publish in line with our values, which are collaborative, imaginative and "shamelessly literary."

All of our subscribers:

- receive a first-edition copy of each of the books they subscribe to
- are thanked by name at the end of our subscriber-supported books
- receive little extras from us by way of thank you, for example: postcards created by our authors

BECOME A SUBSCRIBER,
OR GIVE A SUBSCRIPTION TO A FRIEND

Visit andotherstories.org/subscriptions to help make our books happen. You can subscribe to books we're in the process of making. To purchase books we have already published, we urge you to support your local or favourite bookshop and order directly from them – the often unsung heroes of publishing.

OTHER WAYS TO GET INVOLVED

If you'd like to know about upcoming events and reading groups (our foreign-language reading groups help us choose books to publish, for example) you can:

- join our mailing list at: andotherstories.org
- follow us on Twitter: @andothertweets
- join us on Facebook: facebook.com/AndOtherStoriesBooks
- admire our books on Instagram: @andotherpics
- follow our blog: andotherstories.org/ampersand